Wilberforce: An Activity Book

24 READY TO USE LESSON PLANS

ANDREW EDWARDS AND **FLEUR THORNTON**

Wilberforce: An Activity Book

First Printing: January 2007

ISBN-13: 978-0-89221-672-7
ISBN-10: 0-89221-672-7
Library of Congress Number: 2006909796

Previously published in Great Britain as *William Wilberforce, The Millionaire Child Worked So Hard to Win the Freedom of African Slaves*; Andrew Edwards and Fleur Thornton, authors; Brian Edwards, series editor; by Day One Publications, Leominster, Great Britain, 2006, www.dayone.co.uk.

Design and art direction by Steve Devane. Thanks to Paul Sayer for his invaluable help with the artwork.

Printed in the United States of America

For information regarding author interviews, please contact the publicity department at (870) 438-5288.

Please visit our website for other great titles: www.newleafpress.net

Permission is given to copy the activity pages and associated for use as class or group material

New Leaf Press
A Division of New Leaf Publishing Group

A JOURNEY THROUGH THE LIFE OF
William**Wilberforce**
the abolitionist who changed the face of a nation

by **KEVIN BELMONTE**
Leading Wilberforce scholar and consultant for the movie Amazing Grace

Also available from New Leaf Publishing:
Walk the fascinating pathways and historic halls of England as you re-trace the steps of legendary abolitionist and staunch Christian man of faith William Wilberforce. This full-color, unique guide to Wilberforce's life was written by Dr. Kevin Belmonte, one of the world's leading scholars dedicated to educating the public about William Wilberforce. It includes descriptions of Wilberforce's work on behalf of social justice issues like slavery and the end of poverty, as well as his many achievements, portraits of him and his contemporaries, and photographs of historic sites in England. An excellent and educational tool to bring history to life for educators — for education, travel, or pleasure reading.

ISBN: 0-89221-671-9 • ISBN 13: 978-0-89221-671-0 • Retail:$14.99

Look for arrows in this activity book indicating corresponding page numbers to learn more about Wilberforce.

Meet William Wilberforce

William lived a life of two halves! One half he was a thoughtless man who cared for no one except himself, parties, and gambling; the other half was a life where he loved those in need and felt sad for those who were treated so badly.

Question 1

What changed this man so dramatically?

Question 2

How did the RSPCA (Royal Society for the Protection of Animals) first get started?

Question 3

Would you have kept working on one aim for 50 years just because you felt it was right?

Question 4

How could one man get his country to spend twenty million pounds ($2,400,000,000 in U.S. dollars today) on something he believed in?

Read on to find the answers...

ACTIVITY ANSWERS FOUND ON PAGE 32

For more information see *A Journey through the Life of William Wilberforce*, pages 12-14

A good start to life?

NATIONAL PORTRAIT GALLERY, LONDON

Pictured top: William Wilberforce at the age of 11.

Pictured above: The oak-paneled dining room in William's house.

Pictured right: The black eagle that was the family coat of arms.

A group of young boys screamed as they ran around the corridors of the old house. These were ordinary boys who enjoyed playing among the corridors and rooms of their huge mansion. I say they were ordinary boys, but one of them was to grow up and become a man who was anything but ordinary!

William had a good start to life. He was born on August 24, 1759, in a seaside town called Hull, Yorkshire. His father was a wealthy trader and owned a lot of land around the area. William and his family lived in a large old mansion house on High Street, where delicious meals were served for them in large oak-paneled rooms. As you entered the house, there was a grand staircase in front of you, with a large carved eagle hanging just below the ceiling; this eagle was the family crest. William seemed to have everything he could wish for. At the front and back of the house there were beautiful, neat gardens for him to play in.

In another part of the country there was second boy, also playing. His name was also William – William Pitt. This boy, like Wilberforce, would grow into an extraordinary man. He would be the future Prime Minister and a close friend of Wilberforce.

FAMILY TANGLES

The names of William's parents are hidden in this tangle of letters. Write down all the letters NOT covered by any other letters.

— — — — — —

Rearrange them to find out the name of William's father.

— — — — — —

Write down all the letters that ARE partly covered by other letters.

— — — — — — — —

Rearrange them to find out the name of William's mother.

— — — — — — — —

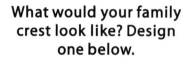
Join the dots to make my family crest.

What would your family crest look like? Design one below.

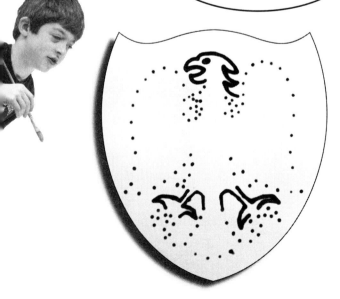

For more information see *A Journey through the Life of William Wilberforce,* pages 15-20

Family troubles

Pictured: *A sign at Hull Grammar School to celebrate the fact that William Wilberforce went there*

From the age of eight William went to Hull Grammar School. It was a very well known school and many famous people had attended it, including people involved in politics and the government. William, being the only boy in his family, was very close to his father and he was very interested in William's education. William enjoyed sports and did well at school.

In the summer of 1768, just before his ninth birthday, William's father died. His eldest sister, Elizabeth, had already died that same year at just 14-years-old. After the death of his father, his mother also became seriously ill. Afraid that she too might die, William was sent to London to live with his uncle and aunt. In London, William was loved and cared for by his uncle and aunt and they had a very important influence on his life. They treated him as if he was their own son and sent William to a private school in Putney which was very strict. William later wrote about how disgusting the food was and complained that he could not eat without sickness!

FACT BOX:
William was so good in school at reading that he was sometimes asked by his teacher to stand on the table and read aloud to the class as an example to his classmates!

His uncle and aunt had a strong Christian faith and often the great preacher John Newton would visit the house and preach to the family. On one occasion John Newton preached a sermon based on *Pilgrim's Progress* – a famous book written by John Bunyan.

FACT BOX:
John Newton used to be the captain of a ship that bought and sold black African slaves. Remember this as you read on. When he became a Christian, Newton's life changed and he began preaching; he later became a Christian minister and wrote hymns. He wrote some famous hymns such as "Amazing Grace."

Unscramble the letters to make two names.

William's aunt

_ _ _ _ _ _

William's uncle

_ _ _ _ _ _ _

Highlight the
words that William used to describe his school master.

"Mr. Chambers the master, himself a Scotch man, had an usher
of the same nation, whose red beard – for he scarcely shaved
once a month – I shall never forget. They taught writing, French,
arithmetic, and Latin ...with Greek we did not much meddle."

How would you describe your school teacher? Be fair!

For more information see *A Journey through the Life of William Wilberforce*, pages 20-23

No more religion for you my lad!

John Newton often used to talk to William about his days at sea and the adventures he had been involved in. The kindness he could see in John and his aunt and uncle began to change the young William. William used to write letters home to his sick mother and tell her of the great sermons he had heard from John. By now, William's mother was recovering well and his grandfather was staying with her to help. She became more and more concerned that William was getting too religious and so the decision was made for William to return back home to his mother and grandfather.

William's mother wanted to make absolutely sure that this religion was gotten rid of, and she decided to focus on teaching him how to be a young gentleman. She would often send him to visit the theater or to dance parties. Sometimes they organized parties themselves and the Wilberforce parties became the talk of the town! At first, William didn't enjoy this lifestyle but after a while he became so popular that he loved all the attention.

William went to the University of Cambridge in October 1776, and had no interest in anything religious at all by this time. He had few morals and could party like the rest of them…. but all that was about to change.

Pictured: William's aunt and uncle, William and Hannah, with whom he stayed in Wimbledon, London. They were evangelical Christians.

FACT BOX:
When William returned home to Hull, he was taught by a man called the Reverend Kingsman Baskett. Mr. Baskett was a real gentleman but treated William to a life of luxury at school because William's family was so wealthy and important. William became the teacher's pet.

What Wiliam said

Follow the letters in the correct order to find out what I said to my aunt and uncle when I had to leave them.

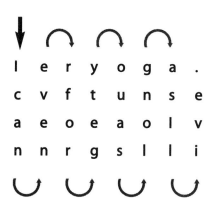

l	e	r	y	o	g	a	.
c	v	f	t	u	n	s	e
a	e	o	e	a	o	l	v
n	n	r	g	s	l	l	i

— — / — — — / — — — — — / — — — — — — /

— — — / — — / — — — — / — — / — /

— — — — .

Could someone say that about you?

Color the dotted areas to find out what William's grandfather called him.

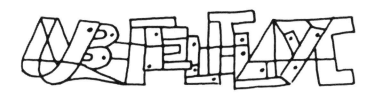

Work out the calculations to discover when William ate

DINNER $\dfrac{(58 \div 2) \times 5 - 1 \div 12}{6}$ O'CLOCK

SUPPER $\dfrac{100}{4} + 5 \times 2 \times \dfrac{1}{10}$ O'CLOCK

A shock and a chosen career

As soon as William arrived at his university and met his fellow classmates he was horrified. Their behavior shocked William so much that even though to start with he joined in, he soon decided he wanted nothing to do with any of them. They would lie, swear, cheat, and get drunk and William was not used to this. Some of them even bullied him and teased him. When he used to work hard on his studies they would laugh and say, "Why in the world should a man of your fortune trouble himself with fagging?" (Fagging was a slang word for boring studies!)

William was one of those annoying people who didn't often have to work hard to be good at what he did. He was very clever and got excellent grades in all his exams just because of this. In the last year of his time at the university he made friends with some very important people. One of these was a young man called… William Pitt. Many of his friends, including Pitt, were the sons of important people in politics who were involved in running the country and making big decisions.

More and more, William felt that he wanted to be a politician. In fact, by the end of his time at the university he had made up his mind. He would not follow in the family business of trading – he would run for Parliament. This chosen career would not make him rich but he didn't need money – he had bags of it from his family.

Pictured: William, just a few years after leaving the university.

FACT BOX:
Having made the decision to become a politician, William worked hard at his studies as he was worried that he would be an embarrassment if he failed.

Spot the difference

There are nine differences — how many can you find?

Picture One

Picture Two

For more information see *A Journey through the Life of William Wilberforce*, pages 28-32

William the politician

William Pitt also started a career in politics. Often both William Pitt and William Wilberforce would sit together in the public gallery of the House of Commons and listen to great debates about important matters in the country.

William Wilberforce was a very warm, friendly person who was able to get on well with almost anyone. This was important in politics and it meant that he was respected by rich and poor people alike. Many of them became his friends. As time went on, listening to all the debates in the House of Commons, William began to feel very interested. He longed to join in with the speeches and debates.

William decided to run for election in his home town of Hull. On one occasion he went into the town to persuade people to vote for him. Someone threw a stone at him and a while later the local butcher came up to speak to William privately. He shook William by the hand and said "I have found out who threw that stone at you, and I'll kill him tonight." William had to try and talk him out of doing this, but the butcher was certain that that was what he was going to do. In the end, William had to compromise with the butcher by saying, "You must only frighten him."

FACT BOX:
One of the great issues being discussed was a war where America, which at this time belonged to Britain, wanted to become an independent country. Both the Williams were against this war and this helped them to become even closer friends together.

William was just 21 years of age when he won the position to stand in Parliament for the City of Hull – this was the youngest you could be to enter Parliament – and so he set off for London.

Pictured: St. Stephen's Tower, part of the the House of Parliament in London (Big Ben is the name of the bell inside the clock, not the tower).

Vote for...

William had to convince the people of Hull to vote for him. If you were standing for election, why would anyone want to vote for you?

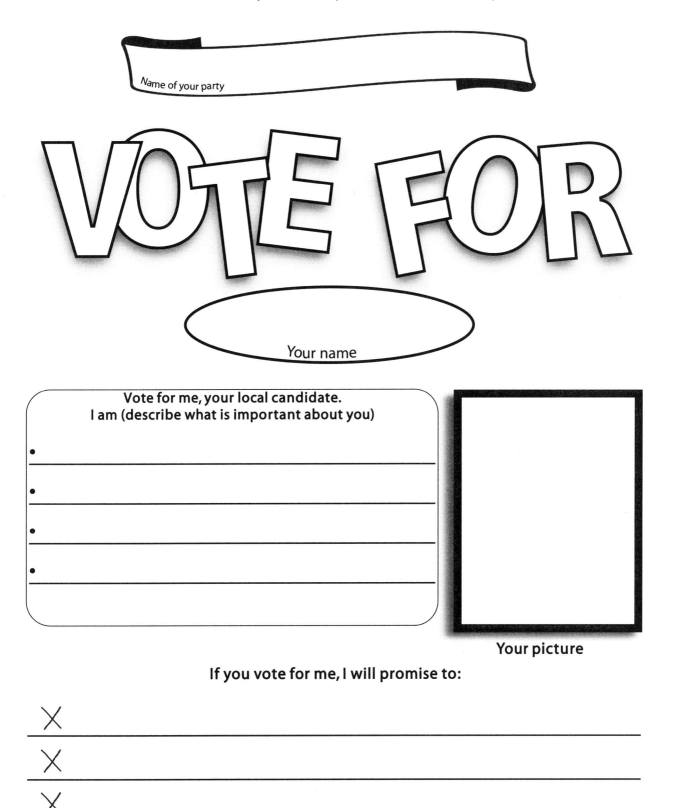

Name of your party

VOTE FOR

Your name

**Vote for me, your local candidate.
I am (describe what is important about you)**

- _____
- _____
- _____
- _____

Your picture

If you vote for me, I will promise to:

X _____
X _____
X _____
X _____

For more information see *A Journey through the Life of William Wilberforce*, pages 32-37

Hey big spender!

William's career in politics went from strength to strength. During the day he was a great politician and at night a singer and gambler! On more than one occasion he lost £100 ($12,000 today) in one go by gambling; once he won more than £600 ($75,000 today) from his friends; unfortunately, they could not afford it and he felt bad. This made him want to stop gambling. By the age of 23, William was in line for promotion. It was planned for him to be made a Lord and take part in debates in the House of Lords in Parliament, however, at the last minute these plans fell through.

William's friend, Pitt, was also doing very well for himself. He had already become a Lord and on December 19, 1783, Pitt became Prime Minister – at only 24 years of age! Wilberforce decided to put himself forward to be a member of Pitt's new Parliament representing the whole of Yorkshire. He won the election and Pitt wrote to him from 10 Downing Street to say, "I cannot congratulate you enough on your glorious success."

Pictured: William Wilberforce *(top) and William Pitt as young Members of Parliament.*

FACT BOX:
In the eighteenth century, politicians would often bribe the public to vote for them or to support them. On one occasion, William held a feast where he roasted a whole cow to try and persuade people that he would make a good candidate!

Traveling to France

During this time, William Wilberforce and William Pitt traveled to France. To find out who they met, write down every 3rd letter. Start with the first letter.

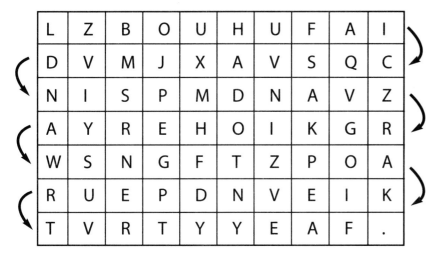

L	Z	B	O	U	H	U	F	A	I
D	V	M	J	X	A	V	S	Q	C
N	I	S	P	M	D	N	A	V	Z
A	Y	R	E	H	O	I	K	G	R
W	S	N	G	F	T	Z	P	O	A
R	U	E	P	D	N	V	E	I	K
T	V	R	T	Y	Y	E	A	F	.

_ _ _ _ _

_ _ _

_ _ _ _ _

_ _ _ _ _ _ _ _ _ _ _ _ _

Count the votes to see who won the election to represent Hull in the House of Commons.

$\times$ = 100 votes

LORD ROBERT MANNERS  = _____ votes

DAVID HARTLEY = _____ votes

WILLIAM WILBERFORCE  = _____ votes

For more information see *A Journey through the Life of William Wilberforce*, pages 38-49

A life-changing debate

Pictured: *John Newton, William's friend who he arranged to meet to discuss the Christian faith.*

William Wilberforce was about to change the world! To celebrate his win in Parliament, William decided to take a vacation. He toured round France and Italy with a friend to keep him company. William had invited his old university teacher Isaac Milner along for the trip. Soon after William had invited Isaac to join him, he discovered that he was a Christian, and the two of them held strongly different opinions on things. Being a politician, William loved debating and discussing, and so he agreed with Milner that they would spend the holiday debating their different views. Unusually for William, he struggled with some of Isaac's debates and the two would spend hours discussing Christianity together. When William returned home in October 1785, he arranged a meeting with the Rev. John Newton, the friend he had got to know in his boyhood, to discuss further some of the questions he had.

This meeting was the turning point in William's life. He decided that he must live his life as a Christian. William shared his decision with Pitt, who was at first afraid that William might now give up politics. Both Pitt and Newton confirmed to William that he could still serve as a politician if he was a Christian. John Newton helped him especially to see that any decisions he made in future years could be based on the Bible and what God says is right.

FACT BOX:
Because of the way so many politicians lived their lives – bribing people, lying, gambling, etc.– William was really not sure if he could continue serving both God and his country. He asked many friends for their opinions on this and they all convinced him that he could. William would now have to be a very different type of politician and everyone would notice!

Secret code

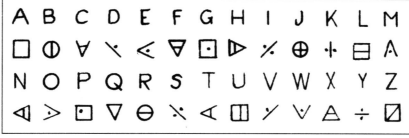

I have written secretly to John Newton asking to meet with him. Use the code to see what I wrote.

A	B	C	D	E	F	G	H	I	J	K	L	M

N	O	P	Q	R	S	T	U	V	W	X	Y	Z

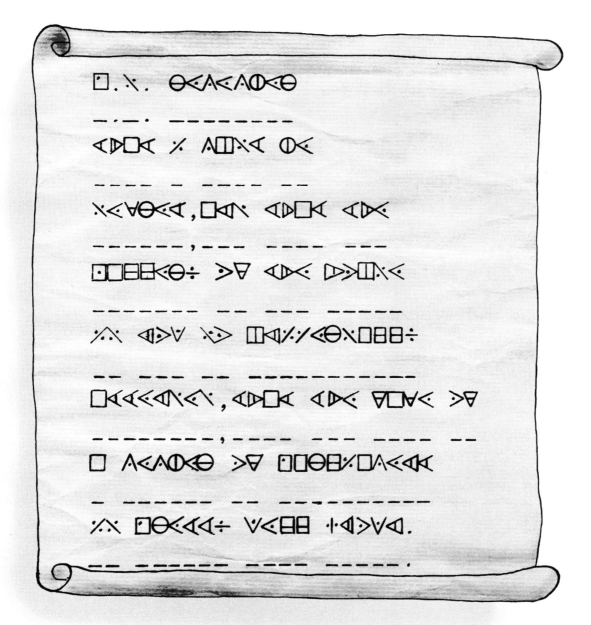

For more information see *A Journey through the Life of William Wilberforce*, pages 50-54

Two weeks to live!

William set his mind on being an honest and good politician. He made up with all the people he had previously upset and everyone who knew him was amazed by the changes in his life.

These were troubled times for Britain. The country had been at war with France for some time and the famous Battle of Waterloo had not yet been fought.

FACT BOX:
Waterloo was a little village eight miles south of Brussels in Belgium where, on June 18, 1815, Wellington defeated the French army under Napoleon Bonaparte, and brought to an end a very long war with France.

FACT BOX:
For two hundred years, British ships sailed to West Africa and captured black people to serve as slaves in the West Indies, North America, and England. These slaves were bought and sold like cows at the market and were mostly treated with great cruelty.

On Sunday, October 28, 1787, William met up with John Newton, and the two friends chatted for a long time together. They talked about all sorts of things and among the conversation they discussed how bad things were in Britain. They discussed the slave trade – an issue which had been on William's mind for a while now.

William felt sure that the slave trade was wrong and that God wanted him to do something about it. He began to speak in Parliament for the trading of slaves to be made illegal but things were going wrong.

By early 1788 William was complaining that he was feeling very unwell. Doctors examined him and said that he had entire decay of all the vital functions and that he had not stamina to last a fortnight. The doctors sent him to Bath as they thought that the mineral water there would be good for him!

While William was at Bath, Pitt made a speech in Parliament and promised to consider the slave trade.

Pictured: *The pump room at Bath as it would have looked when William was there.*

Two goals

God has given me two goals. To find out what they are, rearrange the boxes below.

3 of the	5 trade	4 slave
6 and the	1 The	8 of
2 supression	9 manners	7 reformation

1	2	3
4	5	6
7	8	9

What are you aiming for in your life?
William felt that he had wasted many years of his life by putting himself first.

_____

_____

_____

Murder and death threats

Pictured: The condition of the slaves that William described in Parliament.

William slowly got better and returned to Parliament in 1789 to find that many people were now in favor of abolishing (getting rid of) the slave trade. On May 12 he gave a three-hour speech on the subject. It was an important speech that persuaded many people. During the speech he described what life was like for the slaves and how terrible the conditions were that they were forced to live in. A lot of his information he gained from John Newton, the former slave ship captain.

Speeches and debates continued, and in April 1791, after a four-hour debate, there was a vote in the House of Commons. Eighty-eight members voted to get rid of slavery and one hundred and sixty-three voted to keep slavery. All William's work seemed to have been a waste of time. William made sure that the issue was still debated, though, and in 1792 more support was gained. On one occasion, William named a captain of one ship who had murdered a 15-year-old black slave girl. The captain threatened to kill him, and for a while a friend traveled with him as a bodyguard. Another captain challenged him to a duel (a fight between two men usually to settle a dispute), but William was opposed to this. Throughout his very busy life, William always made Sunday a day of rest and he spent it with his family.

FACT BOX:
Around this time more than seventeen thousand slaves each year were sold at the Royal Exchange in London, and many tens of thousands more in Jamaica and America. Often up to two hundred slaves would be packed below decks in a ship just one hundred feet long (just over 30 meters). In Jamaica and America, slaves were made to work so hard that few lived longer than nine years.

London to Yorkshire

Be the first to get to Yorkshire from London without being attacked by the captains from the slave ships. You will need different colored pieces and a die (one dice!) to tell you how many squares to move forward.

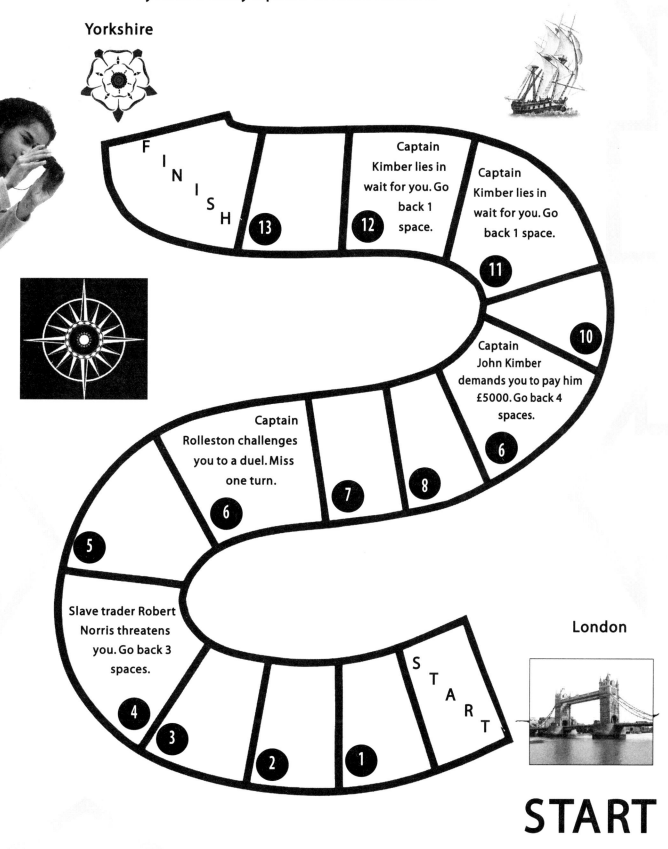

Yorkshire

FINISH

13

12 Captain Kimber lies in wait for you. Go back 1 space.

11 Captain Kimber lies in wait for you. Go back 1 space.

10

Captain John Kimber demands you to pay him £5000. Go back 4 spaces.

6

Captain Rolleston challenges you to a duel. Miss one turn.

6

7

8

5

Slave trader Robert Norris threatens you. Go back 3 spaces.

4

3

2

1

START

London

START

William Wilberforce Wins!

Pictured: *Statue of an unfettered slave at the Pocklington School, near Hull. Wilberforce's memory and legacy is cherished there.*

The debates continued, and time and time again William lost his argument by only a handful of votes. In 1796 he would have clearly won except that so many of his supporters were away at the opera when the vote took place that the measure failed by four votes! All this stress was having an effect on William and he even had to take a short break in the country so that he did not get seriously ill. Every year from 1797–1803 William battled for the law to make slavery illegal and constantly things went wrong. In 1805 another vote took place which had a very close result. Seventy were for the law and seventy-seven against!

In January 1806, William's friend, William Pitt, died and Lord Grenville was made the new Prime Minister. This was good news as Lord Grenville was very strongly against the slave trade. In 1807 there was yet more debate and this time William won. On February 23, 1807, trading in slaves was made illegal. Two hundred and twenty-three people voted for the law and only sixteen against! The House of Commons gave three cheers for Wilberforce – the only time this has happened in the Commons. No longer could slaves be bought and sold like property. Someone present commented that, "They welcomed him with applause such as was scarcely ever before given to any man…."

Unfortunately this was only the end of buying and selling slaves; those who were already slaves could still be kept and used, in fact many were still being treated terribly and William's attention now turned to this and other causes.

FACT BOX:
The debate in Parliament on the slave trade was opened by William in 1798. The slave trade was made illegal in 1807 – in the year John Newton died. The slaves were not set free until 1833 – in the year William died.

What happened to the slaves?

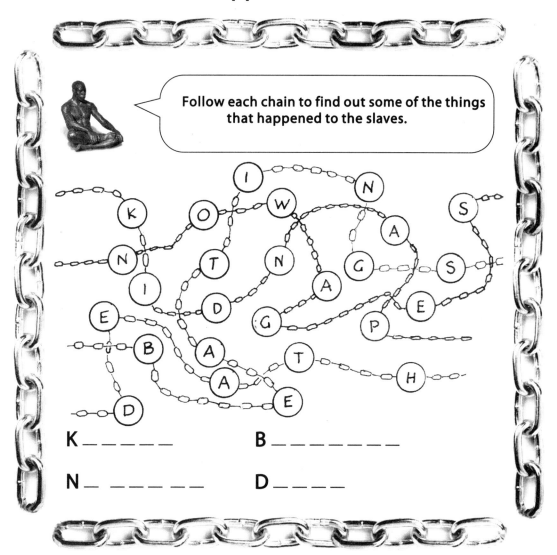

Follow each chain to find out some of the things that happened to the slaves.

K _ _ _ _ _ _   B _ _ _ _ _ _ _ _

N _ _ _ _ _ _   D _ _ _ _

True False

1. **True False** More than 10 million Africans were captured and enslaved.

2. **True False** Approximately ten percent of all the slaves died on the sea journey.

3. **True False** Most of the slaves were shipped to Europe.

4. **True False** Many of the slaves were marked with branding irons.

5. **True False** The Royal Navy sailors said they could smell a slave ship up to 5 miles away.

6. **True False** On some ships the space between decks was reduced from 5ft (1.5m) to 2ft 6in (76cm).

For more information see *A Journey through the Life of William Wilberforce*, pages 64-74

Mind your manners!

William was concerned that there were so few morals in people around him. People in Britain seemed to be able to do and say what they pleased with very little thought for others or, more importantly, for God. To deal with this concern, in 1787 he set up an organization called the Society for the Reformation of Manners – by manners, he meant morals.

William felt that if he set up this organization and others like it then eventually the King and Queen would have to sit and up and take notice. He hoped that they would then force through a law which would encourage people to think more about their actions.

William lived in Clapham in London, and he had a circle of about a dozen friends who were very important people and they were all Christians. Some were bankers and all were wealthy men. This group of friends became known as the Clapham Circle, and they had an enormous influence on the nation at this time.

FACT BOX:
In Britain at this time, hundreds of people were flocking to the cities to get jobs in the newly built factories. Conditions were very poor. Houses were run down and overcrowded. Alcohol was extremely cheap, disease was everywhere, and people were forced to work in dangerous jobs for very little money.

This Clapham Circle set up many voluntary organizations whose main aims were to stand against the bad things that were going on around. Many modern-day charities and organizations have come from these clubs that William and his friends set up. Modern-day lending libraries, schools for the deaf and blind, the RSPCA, schools and colleges where people could learn a trade, groups that would vaccinate people against the deadly smallpox disease, and many others were all set up. It is estimated that William was involved in setting up and running over 70 different charities!

William and change

Split up the words to find out what William believed about change.

Let/r efor m/beg inin myna tion andl etit begi nwit hme

Help the RSPCA by getting the dogs back to the kennels.

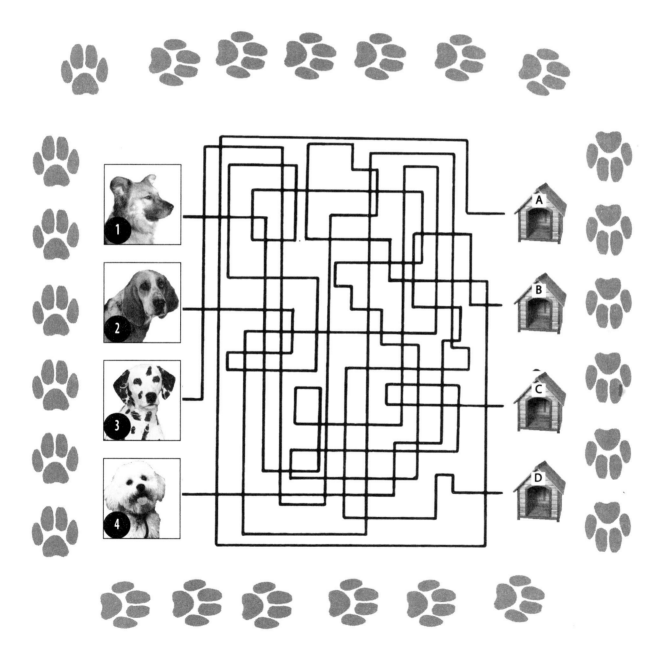

For more information see *A Journey through the Life of William Wilberforce*, pages 75-98

The work grows and so does the family

Pictured: *The house that William and his family lived in between 1808 and 1821.*

In between all this, William personally visited prisons and hospitals. He managed to get people released who had been sent to prison for things such as simply owing money. On one occasion, William heard of a navy officer who had a young family. The officer had been thrown into prison for owing £80 ($9,600 today). William paid his debt, got him released, and used his power to get the man a ship for him to command. Within the year, the young captain returned to visit William with a story to tell. His ship had met an enemy ship, he had captured it and was given promotion in the fleet.

In fact, William's influence even spread abroad. He set up charities to help those who had been affected by war in their countries. He personally made savings wherever he could so that he could give more of his own fortune to the needy and at one point was known to be giving at least a quarter of all the money he earned in a year to the needy.

In 1796 William felt it was time to find a wife. But who should it be? A lady called Barbara Spooner was encouraged to write to William, which she did, and he found her letter charming. Two days later they met and ten days after this William proposed to her! They were married on May 30, 1797. He was 37 and Barbara was only 20, but it was a perfect marriage and they lived happily.

Within ten years of being married, William and Barbara had six children.

FACT BOX:

William born in 1798

Barbara born in 1799

Elizabeth born in 1801

Robert born in 1802

Samuel born in 1805

Henry William born in 1807

William was a great family man who loved his wife and thoroughly enjoyed spending time playing with his children. He still loved his parties, although now, of course, these were much more family occasions.

What was the name of the group that William and the other talented Christian men and women belonged to which campaigned to change many things?

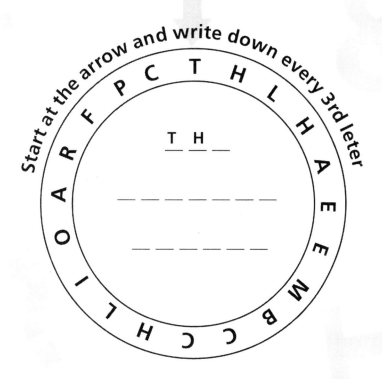

Start at the arrow and write down every 3rd leter

P C T H L H A E E M B C C H L I O A R F

T H _
_ _ _ _ _ _ _
_ _ _ _ _

Find the name of William and Barbara's children in the word search. There are 6 to find.

T	A	Y	V	Z	N	O	I	L	A	F	E
W	M	I	L	L	I	M	H	E	M	L	E
I	A	R	A	B	R	A	B	R	I	Z	L
B	I	O	O	O	Z	H	O	Z	S	G	I
A	L	B	T	B	E	B	B	S	A	A	Z
R	L	T	N	R	B	T	A	M	M	S	A
B	I	E	Y	E	E	M	E	U	L	M	B
A	W	R	R	W	U	B	D	N	G	L	E
E	K	R	B	E	F	G	O	F	T	S	T
M	A	I	L	L	I	W	Y	R	N	E	H

1 _____ -

2 _____ -

3 _____

4 _____ .

5 _____

6 _____

For more information see *A Journey through the Life of William Wilberforce*, pages 98-111

More trouble ahead

On February 22, 1825, William retired from Parliament and shortly after this he bought a beautiful country farm called Highwood Hill complete with about 140 acres of land.

Pictured: *How about this for a garden? Part of the estate at Highwood Hill Farm.*

Even though he had retired from Parliament, William worked hard to end slavery and continue his good works. On May 15, 1830, he led a meeting of the Anti-Slavery Society. By now he was a very weak man. Two thousand people turned up for the meeting and hundreds more had to be turned away at the door.

Sadly, his eldest son got heavily into debt. He owed around £50,000 (over six million dollars today). His father had given so much money away that he could scarcely afford that amount. His friends set up a recovery fund to help him out, but William would only accept money for a church he was building. In the end, William had to leave the farm and estate he loved so much. By the time he left Highwood Hill he was seriously ill and only weighed about 71 pounds, (almost 32 kg). William declared, "I can scarce understand why my life is spared so long, except it be to show that a man can be as happy without a fortune as with one." Shortly afterward their daughter Elizabeth died.

William and Barbara spent their remaining years living with two of their sons who were ministers in the Church of England.

FACT BOX:
William stayed at a place called Brighstone on the Isle of Wight with his son Samuel and his family. William used to love walking over the chalk hills and one particular path was known as "Wilberforce's Down" for many years after.

Can you safely guide William from one son to another?

ROBERT — EAST FARLEIGH

SAMUEL — BRIGHSTONE

For more information see *A Journey through the Life of William Wilberforce*, pages 112-119

A burial with royalty

Living with his son Samuel and his family, William enjoyed watching his grandchildren growing up. On April 20, 1833, William, suffering seriously with flu, visited Bath, but his strength decreased as the illness got worse. He decided to go to London to meet the doctor who had helped him years before.

On the morning of Friday, July 26, William could be found sitting in a chair at the doorway of a house in London, gazing at the trees and grass around him and enjoying the fresh air. The same evening the House of Commons agreed to pay twenty million pounds (over two billion dollars today) for the release of all the slaves in all the countries owned by Britain. On hearing the news, William said, "Thank God that I should have lived to witness a day in which England is willing to give twenty million pounds sterling for the abolition of slavery."

Pictured: *A burial in Westminster Abbey is the highest honor England can give any of its people. William's memorial in Westminster Abbey as it can be seen today.*

For a short while, William seemed to be a little better but the following day his condition got worse and he died at 3:00 in the morning on Monday, July 29, 1833.

William's death was felt by everyone. One of his friends commented on the day of his funeral by saying, "As I came towards Westminster Abbey, every third person I met going about their ordinary business was in mourning."

So well respected was William that when he died, a letter was sent to his family signed by most of the members of the Houses of Parliament requesting that he was to be buried in Westminster Abbey. The letter read:

We the undersigned members of both Houses of Parliament, being anxious upon public grounds to show our respect for the memory of the late William Wilberforce, and being also satisfied that public honours can never be more fitly bestowed than upon such benefactors of mankind, earnestly request that he may be buried in Westminster Abbey; and that we . . . may have permission to attend his funeral.

Color the window

This is the Wilberforce window at Holy Trinity Church, Clapham. Use the code to color it in.

A section of the window also appears on the front cover of this book.

CODE

Pp = purple	R = red	G = green
Bl = blue	Y = yellow	Pk = pink
	Br = brown	

For more information see *A Journey through the Life of William Wilberforce*, pages 120-121

Timeline of William's life

1759 (August 24)   William is born in Hull

1776 (October)   William attends university in Cambridge

1780 (September 11)   William was first elected as a member of Parliament for Hull

1789 (May 12)   William's first great speech in Parliament against the slave trade

1796 (March 15)   William only just loses a vote to make slave trading illegal

1797 (May 30)   William marries Barbara Spooner

1807 (February 23)   Trading in slaves is finally made illegal

1825 (February 22)   William retires from Parliament

1833 (July 29)   William dies in London

1835 (August 5)   William's funeral and burial at Westminster Abbey

ACTIVITY ANSWERS:

pg 5: Father's name: Robert, Mother's name: Elizabeth

pg 7: William's aunt: Hannah/William's uncle: William

pg 9: What William Said:"I can never forget you as long as I live," Grandfather's name for William: Billy, Dinner was at 2 o'clock, Supper was at 6 o'clock

pg 11: 1. no ferris wheel in picture two, 2. missing cloud in picture one, 3. clock face on right of tower different in picture two, 4. no chimney on building in picture two (see left side of picture), 5. missing spire on clocktower in picture two, 6. missing spire on side of building in picture two (see right side of picture), 7. missing spire on the upper corner of the clocktower in picture two, 8. missing pole in picture two (see left side of picture), 9. missing notches on roof in picture two (see left side of picture)

pg 15: They met: Louis XVI, Marie Antoinette, Lord Manners - 673 votes, D. Hartley - 453 votes, W. Wilberforce - 1,126 votes

pg17: Secret letter:"P.S. Remember that I must be secret, and that the gallery of the house is now so universally attended, that the face of a member of parliament is pretty well known."

pg19: The supression of the slave trade and the reformation of manners.

pg 23: **K**idnap, **B**eatings, **N**o wages, **D**eath, 1. True, 2. True, 3. False - they were taken to the Americas, 4. True, 5. False - up to 10 miles away, 6. True

pg 25: "Let reform begin in my nation and let it begin with me," Dog 1-kennel D, Dog 2-kennel C, Dog 3-kennel A, Dog 4-kennel B

pg 27: The Clapham Circle

1. Barbara
2. Elizabeth
3. Henry William
4. Robert
5. Samuel
6. William

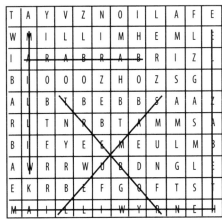

pg 29:

START   FINISH